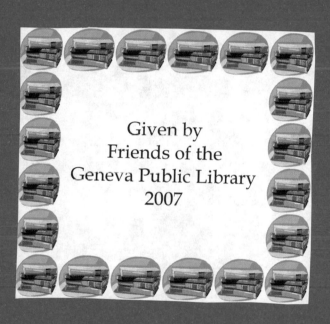

The Bee Tree

by Stephen Buchmann
and Diana Cohn

illustrated by Paul Mirocha

THERE will be no moon tonight.
The honey hunt begins.

ALL the years of my life, I remember my grandfather going to
collect the honey from the bees in the tualang trees. The bees
travel hundreds of miles, even over oceans, and arrive every year
just as the rainforest flowers begin to bloom. We call the tualang
tree near my village the bee tree. It is so tall, I cannot see the top.
Grandfather first learned to climb the bee tree when he was my
age. That is when he fell in love with the bees. In October and
November, Grandfather does not sleep well until he knows that
his "little friends" have returned to build their nests. By the new
moon in February, their combs are full, thick with golden honey.

Everyone calls Grandfather Pak Teh. *Pac de* He is a farmer. I walk by his rice paddies on my way home from school. After my morning lessons, when the call-to-prayer sounds from the *mawsk* mosque behind Grandfather's house, he leads us in prayer. I feel close to Grandfather when we pray.

Ever since I was six years old, I have followed Grandfather into the rainforest. He is the leader of our honey hunting clan, and he tells everyone what their job will be. Some will carry ropes, others will carry leather pails where the honey will be poured, and others will carry the tightly wound vines bundled together for our torches. For the past seven years, my job has been to carry the ropes and leather pails.

Grandfather has the place of honor in the honey hunting clan for he is the one who climbs all the way up the bee tree to gather the honey. "One of you will take my place someday," Pak Teh said during one of the honey harvests. I have wondered all these years if it might be me.

ONE day when he was preparing for the honey hunt, he said, "Nizam, I believe you are the one."

To prove myself, I must climb 120 feet into the sky—to where the first branches unfurl themselves and where the bees make their nests.

Am I brave enough?

Am I strong enough?

I have practiced the climb many times but only during the day. For the honey hunt, we climb in the black of night. At least then I won't see how far it is to the ground below.

At sunrise, we are up and preparing for our journey to the forest. I hear my uncle call from a distance, "Peace be upon you, Pak Teh. Peace be upon you, Nizam." As the rest of the clan arrives, we gather all the supplies we will need for the hunt.

GRANDFATHER touches his heart as he enters the dense rainforest. We hear the familiar chorus of the cicadas and watch the red and silver leaf monkeys move quickly from one tree branch to another. "Remember, Nizam, this is not our forest," he says.

My eyes adjust to the darkness.

Grandfather says, "This forest belongs to the Unseen Protector and if we bring peace in our hearts, the Unseen Protector will look after us like he watches over the forest."

"Yes," I answer, remembering the lesson Grandfather has taught me. "We enter the forest as if visiting a neighbor's home."

WHEN we get to the base of the bee tree, it is so tall that I have to arch my head so it sits on the back of my neck just to see the highest branches. I put my forehead against the smooth bark and stretch my arms wide, touching my fingertips to the hard-as-rock tree. I pray to the Unseen Protector that my arms and legs and heart will be as strong tonight. Grandfather gazes upward at the giant, half-moon-shaped honeycombs, each fat with honey.

"Seventy-eight, seventy-nine, eighty combs," he counts.

AFTER sunset, all of the honey hunters gather around Grandfather while he tells the traditional story of the bees:

Long ago, a beautiful servant girl named Hitam Manis worked in the Sultan's palace. She and the Sultan's son fell in love. He called her "Sweet Dark One." But it was forbidden for a prince to marry any other than a princess, so when the Sultan heard of their love, he was furious. He ordered his soldiers to chase the servant girl from his kingdom.

HITAM Manis fled with her loyal friends. As they ran, a metal spear struck Hitam Manis. The Sweet Dark One fell, but she did not die. A miracle happened. Hitam Manis and the other servant girls were transformed into a swarm of bees. They disappeared together into the forest.

BECAUSE she had been hit by a metal spear, Hitam Manis ruled, "No metal must touch our honey, ever—the person who uses metal must die!"

Years later, the prince was out hunting. He noticed honey combs draping off a tree limb. He climbed up with a pail and cut a chunk of the comb with his knife, but when the pail was lowered to the ground, the other hunters were horrified to see their prince had been cut into little pieces.

From the treetops came the beautiful voice of Hitam Manis. "This man has broken our law!"

But when Hitam Manis realized the man was the prince she once loved, a shower of her golden tears fell into the bucket and the Prince was restored to his former self.

"And that is why," Grandfather says, "we harvest honey without metal, using only a bone knife, a wooden ladder, and a leather pail."

"And," my uncle says, "we respect Hitam Manis and the girl servants as the spirits of the bees."

"Yes," Grandfather smiles, "and we honor them by calling them…"

"Our fine friends!" I say, eager to prove I know the ways of the hunters.

AFTER dark, we gather at the base of the bee tree to pray. We ask the Unseen Protector to guide us. We tell Hitam Manis we are on our way to gather her honey.

"Come, Nizam," Grandfather says, putting his arm around my shoulder. "You have practiced the climb many times and tonight you're ready to meet the bees. I was scared the first time, too, but when I finally reached the honey, it was like a magic spell, making me return again and again to climb the bee tree. Follow me and see if the magic is waiting there for you, as well."

Grandfather lights the torch and ties its cord to his leg. He climbs the wooden ladder barefoot like a long-legged spider. I follow. I climb twenty feet up the tree. I stop, clinging to the ladder. How can I climb another hundred feet?

"It's okay, Nizam," Grandfather says, "just one step at a time, you can do it."

Again I begin climbing one rung after another. I climb to thirty feet, then to forty, then up…and up…and up…and up… I imagine Grandfather's kind eyes looking at me as I climb the next few rungs. I never look down. Grandfather pulls me next to him when I reach the first branch.

"I made it!" I pant.

WE rest, lying along the slender limb. The first nest, almost
six feet wide, is below us.

"They know just where to build their nests," Grandfather says, "so
if the branch is strong enough for the bees, it is strong enough for us."

"Send up the bucket," Grandfather calls down. "Now it is time, Nizam."

We tap the glowing torch against the tree branch just above the first nest, creating a cascade of yellow-orange sparks—falling stars. Once the sparks begin to fly…so do tens of thousands of giant angry buzzing bees. The bees make a deafening sound, like a huge engine. I cover my head with my arms. "Please, Hitam Manis," I pray, "do not sting me!"

THE bees roar past like a raging monsoon, swarming after the glowing sparks falling to the ground.

Below, one of the clan chants,

Turun Hitam Manis!
Come down…Hitam Manis!
Turun dengan cahaya bintang!
Come down with the falling stars!
Turun dengan lemah lembutnya
Come down gracefully!

Once the bees land on the shrubs below, they remain until dawn when the sun rises, when they can see again to find their way home. Until then, we are safe to harvest. This is the honey hunters' secret.

Quiet returns.

WHILE the nest is unguarded, we begin. My bone knife slides right through the thick comb. Holding the comb in my hand is like discovering a treasure chest of gold. I taste the sweet sticky honey and the smell of the beeswax and honey calms me. I feel peaceful for the first time. Is this the magic Grandfather spoke about? I think it must be. I fill the bucket, careful not to let any of the liquid gold spill. My uncles pull the bucket down and send an empty bucket up.

Throughout the night, I move from nest to nest working to the rhythm of the ancient songs. Each time the taps of our torch awaken the bees from their slumber, chants are sung to soothe our "fine friends" as they follow the sparks to the ground.

It is almost dawn when we climb down the bee tree. Grandfather picks a honeycomb and throws it deep into the forest.

"For hundreds of years, we have always given the first honey back to the forest," he says. Grandfather touches his heart. "Now it's your turn, Nizam, to offer some honey to the forest."

I choose a comb dripping with honey. "I think the Unseen Protector will like this one," I say.

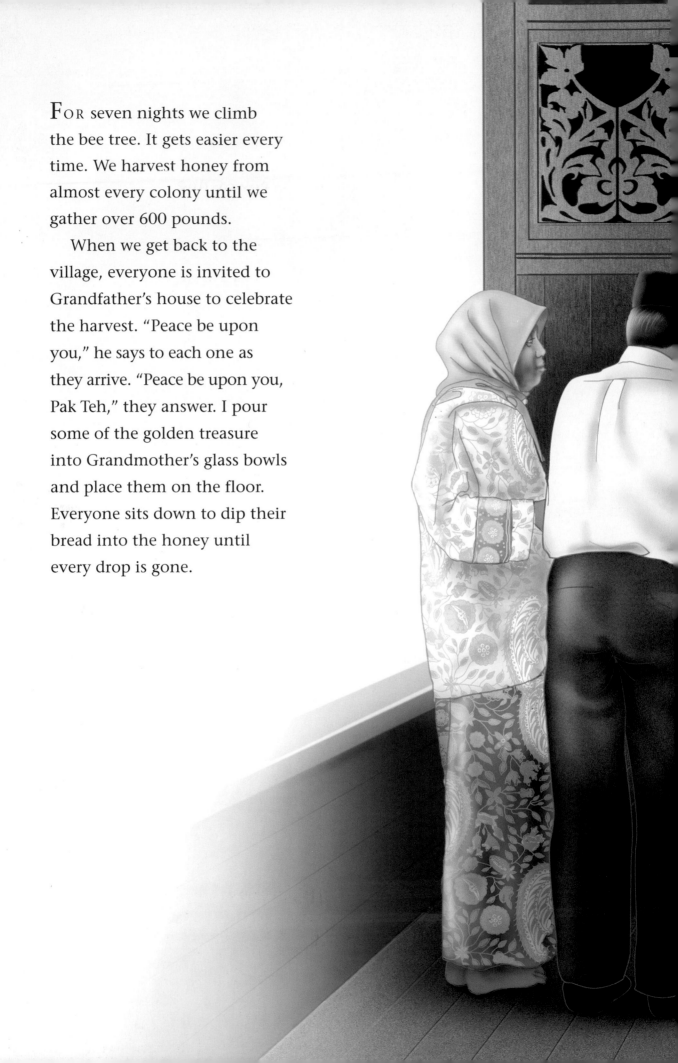

FOR seven nights we climb
the bee tree. It gets easier every
time. We harvest honey from
almost every colony until we
gather over 600 pounds.

   When we get back to the
village, everyone is invited to
Grandfather's house to celebrate
the harvest. "Peace be upon
you," he says to each one as
they arrive. "Peace be upon you,
Pak Teh," they answer. I pour
some of the golden treasure
into Grandmother's glass bowls
and place them on the floor.
Everyone sits down to dip their
bread into the honey until
every drop is gone.

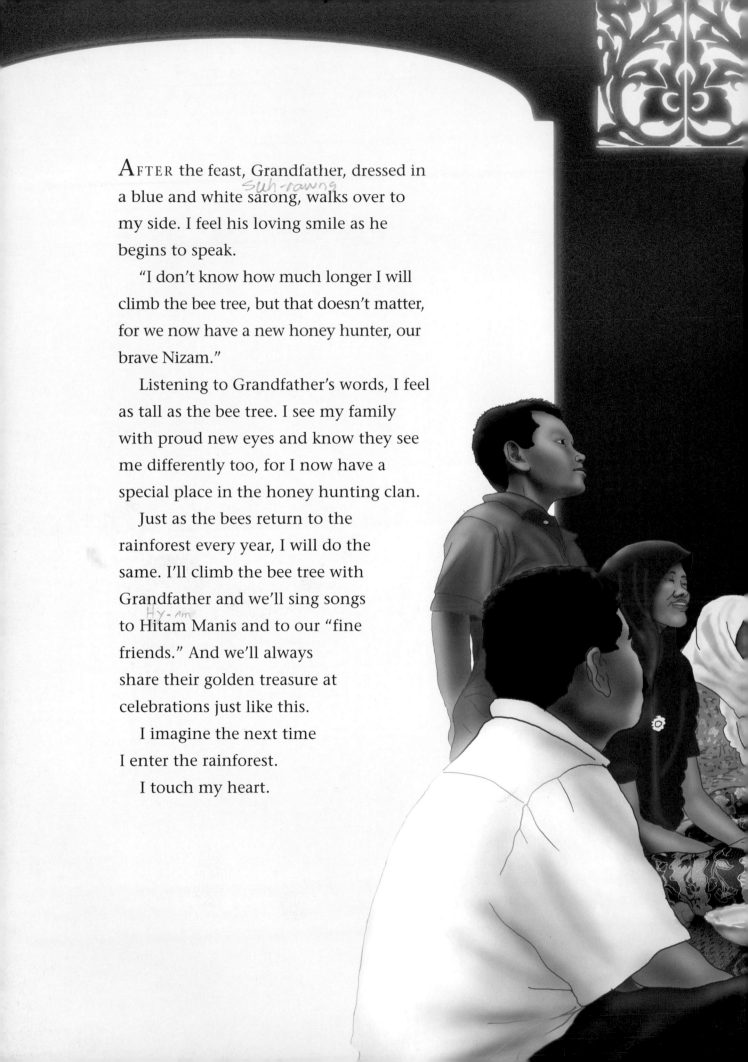

AFTER the feast, Grandfather, dressed in
a blue and white sarong, walks over to
my side. I feel his loving smile as he
begins to speak.

"I don't know how much longer I will
climb the bee tree, but that doesn't matter,
for we now have a new honey hunter, our
brave Nizam."

Listening to Grandfather's words, I feel
as tall as the bee tree. I see my family
with proud new eyes and know they see
me differently too, for I now have a
special place in the honey hunting clan.

Just as the bees return to the
rainforest every year, I will do the
same. I'll climb the bee tree with
Grandfather and we'll sing songs
to Hitam Manis and to our "fine
friends." And we'll always
share their golden treasure at
celebrations just like this.

I imagine the next time
I enter the rainforest.

I touch my heart.

Malaysia

***Tak kenal, tak cinta:* You can't love what you don't know**

—A Malaysian proverb

Pak Teh and Mak Teh gaze from the window of their 100-year-old traditional Malay wood house in Jitra.

We, the creators of *The Bee Tree*, can attest to the truth of this lovely Malaysian proverb, adding from our own experience, though, that you can't really know another culture until someone from that culture invites you in. For we never would have come to love Malaysia without the many fine friends who introduced us to their world, including the honey hunters who gave us our first experience of the magical honey hunt. They were our hosts as we entered the dense rainforest and witnessed the ancient honey-hunting ceremonies on a dark moonless night, an awesome experience unlike anything we had ever had before. This was a precious gift. We offer this book in gratitude to the world's honey hunters of the past, present and future. And we present it to you in hopes that you will come to love Malaysia as we do.

Now, let us tell you more—

Malaysia and its Peoples

Malaysia is a country in Southeast Asia. To get there from the U.S., we had to fly over the Pacific Ocean. Our flight from Los Angeles, California to the capital of Malaysia, Kuala Lumpur, took almost 20 hours. Malaysia is an unusual country because it is composed of two distinct parts separated by the South China Sea. West Malaysia is a peninsula connected on its north with Thailand. East Malaysia sits on the north of the giant forested island of Kalimantan (Borneo) which it shares with Indonesia. The peninsula and the island share a largely similar landscape and environment—hillsides and waterways clothed in deep green rainforest trees.

The mountainous rainforest around Pedu Lake.

Malaysia is a country with over 24 million people from many different cultures. Indigenous people, Indians, Malays, and the Chinese are all Malaysian citizens. Our friends Pak Teh and Nizam are Malays. They live in West Malaysia. The 2 million indigenous people, called "Orang Asli"—which means forest people—live primarily in East Malaysia. Many of the Orang Asli are also traditional honey hunters just like those in *The Bee Tree*. Most Malaysians speak Bahasa Melayu, the country's official language. Their language is similar to that spoken on the hundreds (maybe thousands) of islands which make up the nation of Indonesia.

With so many different kinds of people, Malaysia has an exciting and vibrant cultural life. Our senses were delighted as we walked through the streets and open-air markets. Women wore beautiful silk scarves. Both men and women were wearing sarongs made from cotton or silk, and blouses and shirts with intricate patterns and bold colors. We tried all kinds of new food—tasty chicken satay on bamboo skewers, spicy hot food with different ocean fish or beef, rice flavored with cumin, lemon grass, coconut milk and wild ginger.

Islam is the official religion of the country. The golden spires of mosques rise up like flowers in the midst of cities, towns and countryside. There are beautiful Hindu and Buddhist temples too. Five times a day—at sunrise, noon, mid-afternoon, sunset and after dark—we heard the call to prayer sounding from the mosques.

The tualang trees (Koompassia excelsa) are the tallest trees in the Malaysian rainforest. They can rise to heights of 250 feet, as tall as a thirty-story skyscraper. The trees are rarely felled for lumber because the honey from the bees is regarded as food and medicine.

The Rainforest, the Jewels of the Earth

Our hosts led us into the rainforest along a narrow trail that wound its way uphill from the road to the bee tree. The air here was thick with moisture and afternoon heat. Since Malaysia is close to the equator, there aren't true seasons, only wet and less wet times of the year.

We felt as if we were entering a giant cathedral—the tree trunks were like thick brown pillars holding up a leafy green roof that blocked out the sun. Looking down along the trail, we saw splotches of color: yellows, whites, pinks and blues. These were the petals of countless flowers that rain down upon the forest floor from above.

Rainforests are miraculous places where an abundance of plants— trees, shrubs, herbs, vines, mosses—create a flowering cornucopia of colors and smells. Over 750 species of trees can be found in just twenty-five acres (roughly the size of twenty-five football fields) of Malaysian

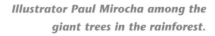
Illustrator Paul Mirocha among the giant trees in the rainforest.

rainforest. That's more tree species than in all the continental United States, where there are 600 species. It's hard to imagine so many kinds of trees. Each one has a slightly different bark, leaves and flowers. We will never encounter so many different trees as we did on the hillsides above Pedu Lake.

This exotic environment provides wonderful habitat for an almost infinite variety of birds, mammals, reptiles and insects. Indeed, rainforests are home to two-thirds of all the living animal and plant species on the planet. Scientists believe that they still have tens of millions of new species of plants, insects and microorganisms to discover in these forests!

The rainforest has multiple stacked layers of plants, beginning with the forest floor and stretching to the upper reaches of the tallest trees. Young forest trees strain and grow to be the first to reach the

light at the top of the forest, the upper canopy. Too much shade can stunt or kill plants that remain below, so the forest floor is nearly bare. Fungi and insects quickly eat all the leaves that fall to the ground. Woody vines, called lianas, wrap around trees and make their way up into the canopy.

Insects are the most common creatures that live in the forest—butterflies with iridescent wings, dragonflies, colorful beetles, cicadas with their shrill cries and green katydids, to name only a few. Some insects are brilliantly colored, while others—camouflaged like leaves, twigs or thorns—play hide and seek amid the foliage. Though some insects are silent, we heard others all around us, though we didn't always see them.

In the Malaysian rainforests of our story, giant mammals—tigers, Asian elephants and the Malaysian tapir—roam in the darkness of the forest floor. At dawn and dusk, we heard noisy gibbons "sing" beautiful duets together to announce their presence. Above in the

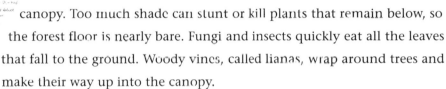

trees, three-foot-long flying squirrels and gliding lizards leapt from branch to branch. Monkeys of every variety ate the leaves and fruits of the tall trees. Many will spend their entire lives in the treetops. Below them live frogs, lizards, snakes, deer, river otters, bizarre birds and snakes—including the venomous King Cobra.

Now we know firsthand why the rainforests are called the "jewels of the earth."

*If you want to learn more about the rainforest plants and animals of Malaysia, please visit the website of the Malaysian Nature Society at **www.mns.org.my***

Giant Honey Bees

There are more than 20,000 kinds of bees in the world. Surprisingly, most of them do not make honey! There are only about 660 kinds of bees that make honey. These include bumble bees, stingless bees and true honey bees. Many true honey bees are domesticated, kept by beekeepers in white hive boxes, like our familiar European honey bees. Honey bees store surplus honey in their wax combs, making it easy for people to harvest. This is the honey sold in farmers markets and on supermarket shelves.

Many *wild* honey bees live in the tall Asian rainforests. The giant honey bee, called *Apis dorsata*, is the world's largest honey-maker. The bees are one inch long, with colorful bands of orange, black and brown, and have smoky dark wings. They make their nests under the wide branches of the tallest trees, especially the tualang trees. The bees make beeswax which they shape into huge two-sided combs. Their nests hang like half-moons under the protective tree branches. Each comb is six feet across and three or four feet wide! Thirty thousand or more giant honey bees live on the surface of the nest.

© Stephen Buchmann

Giant honey bees don't live in tree hollows or bee hives. Their single comb wax nests are attached under tree branches. Right: Several layers deep, their bodies form a living "bee blanket" protecting the delicate wax nest from wind, rain and predators.

© Stephen Buchmann

Their hairy bodies form a living "bee blanket" several bees deep—it keeps the nests dry even during a monsoon downpour.

The most amazing thing about these Asian honey bees is their migration as a colony from place to place—following the new blooms—to harvest nectar and store it as honey. Each October or November in the forests surrounding Pedu Lake in Peninsular Malaysia, the migrating bees arrive at the bee trees and build new wax nests. Pak Teh is happy when he finds the first nests of the year up in the bee tree.

Nobody knows where the migrating bees go when they leave every year, but like the salmon or the Monarch butterflies, they somehow find their way back home. The bees often return to the same branch of their special tree every year. And this is even more amazing when you consider that only the queen bee is long-lived—the other bees are not the same bees who left the branch the year before.

Some bee trees have been found with more than one hundred active bee nests! The honey hunters can collect as much as one thousand pounds of delicious wild honey from a single tree.

The giant honey bees vigorously defend their nests against people and other animals. Pak Teh taught us that when you walk around the base of a bee tree, you must walk slowly and hide your movements beneath bushes and small trees. Many people who don't take these precautions are stung each year, attacked by hundreds of bees flying down from their nests.

During our first honey hunt, when the sparks flew down from the torches held by the honey hunters and the bees chased them to the ground, we instinctively ducked and covered our faces with our hands—the bees created a loud roar that terrified us. The honey hunters stay safe because they climb the trees for honey only on moonless nights. In the darkness, the bees cannot find them to sting.

Author Stephen Buchmann with Pak Teh on the forest edge, as they pause before hiking uphill to the bee tree at Pedu Lake.

Honey Hunters

"Everything in the forest is given by the Creator, and it is for us to make use of, but we must preserve whatever is given by the Creator. We need to take care of the forest and if we do so, the forest will take care of us." —Pak Teh

Pak Teh holds the big leather pail (honey bucket) and the bone knife used for harvesting the honey combs.

Early peoples discovered that true honey bees store up enough honey to make it worthwhile to collect the honey from their wild hives. For thousands of years, mostly in hot humid tropical countries where honey bees are abundant, people have climbed trees and scaled cliffs, suffering the painful stings of angry bees protecting their nests, to get at the sweet golden honey. The delicious honey—a nutritious food which supplies energy quickly to our bodies—is their reward. The honey is also used for medicine. The honey hunters put it on burns and wounds to keep them germ-free and to help them heal faster.

The Orang Asli—the indigenous people of Malaysia—as well as traditional Malays have always been skilled honey hunters. The honey hunt is central to their culture and way of life. Just as in *The Bee Tree*, the honey hunters climb only on moonless nights or after the moon has set. They climb the tall tualang trees using a special wooden ladder and ropes.

The honey hunters construct a thin but strong wood ladder (some say it looks like fish bones) up the straight smooth trunk of the tualang tree and out onto its massive branches.

We were amazed at the skill and courage required in hunting honey. One time, we bravely tried climbing up the bee tree ladder about 15 feet so we could take each other's photo. That was enough for us. The idea of climbing the flimsy ladder another 100 plus feet was more than we could stand.

The honey hunters have a deep respect for the animals and plants of the forest. They sing prayers to the bees while they harvest the honey. Using their liana torches, the honey hunters tap the branches above each nest, sending a cascade of bright orange sparks floating slowly to the ground. The bees chase the sparks and remain on the ground below until dawn, when the sun rises and the bees can again see to fly. With all the bees on the ground, the honey hunters are safe to cut the honey combs high above.

After harvesting the honey, the hunters share their bounty with their friends and neighbors from their village. They also sell this honey in local markets. The honey hunters' wild honey is the very finest and continues to be held in the highest esteem throughout Malaysia.

The Future

Because we were invited to participate in the honey hunt, we saw firsthand how Pak Teh is keeping this ancient tradition alive. When we asked him what the future is for honey bees, the Malaysian honey hunters and the world's oldest rainforests, he answered, "As long as there is the rainforest, there will be bees, and as long as there are bees, there will be honey, and as long as there is honey, there will be honey hunters." Pak Teh has been teaching the young people in his village—like Nizam and other young men his age—the ways of the honey hunt so that the gathering of the honey will continue.

Bee Tree

The mighty tualang, or the bee trees, are "trees of life," their branches home to many other rainforest animals and plants. Every day, scientists discover new species of plants and animals in these forests. Many of these plants contain powerful new medicines that can help cure the peoples of the world.

But even more important to the honey hunters is the fact that the *Apis dorsata*, the giant honey bee, is crucial as a pollinator of many of the rainforest trees and other plants. To imagine its importance, think of an arch made of stone. At the very top of the arch is a stone called the keystone. This stone has the least pressure on it of any of the stones in the arch, but if it is taken out, the arch will collapse.

The giant honey bee is like that keystone. In fact, it's known as a keystone species, a species on which the existence of a large number of other plants and animals in the rainforest depends. Without the honey bee, the rainforest and the entire ecosystem it upholds would fail. Knowing this and having had the privilege to enter the rainforest as the guests of the honey hunters, we understand the great reverence and honor they pay these fierce, buzzing creatures as they gather the rich healing honey from their nests.

—*Stephen Buchmann, Diana Cohn and Paul Mirocha*

© Paul Mirocha

Author Diana Cohn with a new friend at Desa Utara on the shores of Pedu Lake.

We dedicate this book to those who cherish and celebrate the bees and the forests — the honey hunters of the past, present and future.

Acknowledgments

Our heartfelt thanks to our rain forest guide, mentor and favorite honey hunter, Salleh bin Mohammed Noor, also known as Pak Teh.

We respectfully acknowledge the Sultan of Kedah State, His Royal Highness Tuanku Sultan Haji Abdul Halim Mu'adzam Shah ibni Al-Marhum Sultan Badlishah for his protection of the forests, their flowers and the bee trees.

A very special *terima kasih banyak banyak* (thank you very much) to our dear friend and mentor, Professor Dato' Dr. Makhdzir bin Mardan of the Universiti Putra Malaysia, and Noor Azhar bin Zainal of the Putrajaya Botanical Gardens.

A bouquet of flowers for Mariam binti Bakar (respectfully known as Mak Teh) for opening her home to us; and to her grandsons Nizam bin Mustapha and Shukor bin Ayob.

A shower of falling stars for the honey hunters from the village of Jitra: Hamdan bin Ariffin, Ayob bin Arshad, Kob bin Haji Bakar, Mohammed Naim bin Ayob, Mohammed Hafiz bin Ahmad, Majid bin Mohammed Arif, Haji Hashim bin Haji Mohammed Rejab, Yaakob bin Bakar, Shaari bin Ismail, Ku Ibrahim, Hazizan, and Ali.

Bread dipped in honey for our friends on the staff of the Desa Utara eco-resort at Pedu Lake, especially Hamid bin Harun and Roslan bin Abdul Karim; to Abdul Razak (known as Mat) for his help with logistics; for Mohammed Hasdiman M. Hasim (known as Man) for taking us on botanical tours of the forest, Amir Abdul Wahab for hosting Paul at his home in the Kampung, and Aslina Ahmad for posing as Hitam Manis.

A beeswax candle for Rosli bin Abu Bakar of the State Tourism Division of the Economic Planning Unit, and to the Office of the State Secretary of the Kedah State Government. We are grateful to the Federal Agricultural Marketing Authority (FAMA), the organization which markets and helps sell *Apis dorsata* honey produced by the honey hunters in Kedah.

A piece of the first honey comb in respect to the spirits of the ancestors—human, plant and animal—who came to the forest before us.

Lastly we give our thanks to those who over many years supported the creation of this book including Bobby and Lee Byrd and Vicki Trego Hill of Cinco Puntos Press; our literary agent Scott Treimel; Laurie Adams, Melanie Adcock, Jennifer Beckman, Etienne Boeuf, Marlyse and Melissa Buchmann, Lynne Cherry, Arthur Donovan, Jo Duranceau, Lisa Futterman, Alie Ghiorse, Shelly Gillum, Paul Growald, Paul Hawken, Barbara Kingsolver, Rhod Lauffer, Josh Mailman, Anna and Claire Mirocha, Chester Mirocha, Julie Mirocha, Gary Paul Nabhan, Patricia Philbin, Judith Riven, Hans Schoepflin, David Schwartz, Nikos Valance, Mary Woltz; and finally, to Patricia Cowan, Christina Robinson, and Craig Merrilees for their daily encouragement and belief in this project.

Visit us at **www.cincopuntos.com** or call 1-800-566-9072

Book & cover design & art direction by Vicki Trego Hill of El Paso, Texas. Printed in Hong Kong by Morris Press & Creative Printing, U.S.A.

Copyright © 2007 by Stephen Buchmann and Diana Cohn. Illustrations copyright © 2007 by Paul Mirocha. All rights reserved. No part of this book may be used or reproduced in any manner whatsoever without written permission except in case of brief quotations for reviews. For information, write Cinco Puntos Press, 701 Texas, El Paso, TX 79901 or call at (915) 838-1625. Printed in Hong Kong.

FIRST EDITION   10   9   8   7   6   5   4   3   2   1

Library of Congress Cataloging-in-Publication Data. Buchmann, Stephen L. The bee tree / by Stephen Buchmann and Diana Cohn ; with illustrations by Paul Mirocha. — 1st ed.   p. cm. Summary: In the rain forests of Malaysia, Nizam waits anxiously to climb the bee tree, proving that he is capable of succeeding his grandfather as leader of the traditional honey-hunting clan.   ISBN-13: 978-0-938317-98-2 / ISBN-10: 0-938317-98-9 (alk. paper) [1. Bees—Fiction. 2. Coming of age—Fiction. 3. Malaysia—Fiction.] I. Cohn, Diana. II. Mirocha, Paul, ill. III. Title. PZ7.B877325Bee 2007 [Fic]—dc22   2006023349